香港國際詩歌之夜 *2015*
INTERNATIONAL POETRY NIGHTS IN HONG KONG

編輯 Editors

北島 Bei Dao

陳嘉恩 Shelby K. Y. Chan

方梓勳 Gilbert C. F. Fong

柯夏智 Lucas Klein

馬德松 Christopher Mattison

宋子江 Chris Song

中文翻譯：宋子江

目錄 Contents

萊斯·馬雷
Les Murray

Kiss of the Whip

In Cardiff, off Saint Mary's Street,
there in the porn shops you could get
a magazine called Kiss of the Whip.
I used to pretend I'd had poems in it.

Kiss of the Whip. I never saw it.
I might have encountered familiar skills
having been raised in a stockwhip culture.
Grandfather could dock a black snake's head,

Stanley would crack the snake for preference
leap from his horse grab whirl and jolt!
the popped head hummed from his one-shot
  slingshot.
The whips themselves were black, fine-braided,

arm-coiling beasts that could suddenly flourish
and cut a cannibal strip from a bull
(millisecond returns) or idly behead an
ant on the track. My father did that.

A knot in the lash would kill a rabbit.
There were decencies: good dogs and children
were flogged with the same lash doubled back.
A horsehair plait on the tip for a cracker

sharpened the note. For then or twelve thousand
years this was the sonic barrier's
one human fracture. Whip-cracking is that:
thonged lightning making the leanest thunder.

When black snakes go to Hell they are
affixed by their fangs to carved whip-handles
and fed on nothing but noonday heat,
sweat and flowing rumps and language.

They writhe up dust-storms for revenge
and send them roaring where creature comfort's
got with a touch of the lash. And that
is a temple yard that will bear more cleansing

before, through droughts and barracks, those
lax, quiet-speaking, sudden fellows
emerge where skill unbraids from death
and mastering, in Saint Mary's Street.

吻鞭

卡迪夫城，聖瑪麗街邊
情色舖林立，你能找到
一本雜誌，叫《吻鞭》。
我常常假裝自己在雜誌上面發表了詩歌。

《吻鞭》。我從未見過。
我可能曾經見過熟悉的技巧
畢竟我是在牧鞭文化中長大。
祖父還會用鞭抽起一條黑蛇的頭，

史丹利能用鞭隨意抽打蛇身
還抓著馬繩跳下，跑圈顛簸！
蛇頭被擊中，鞭準下嗚咽。
鞭身是黑色的，編結得不錯，

猶如叉起手臂的野獸，突然活躍起來
從一頭公牛身上抽出人食的肉條
（毫秒間回頭）或休憩中抽斷
蟻隊中螞蟻的頭。我父親就幹過。

鞭子打結就能絞死一隻兔子。
當中亦有得體之處：聽話的狗和孩子
都被同一條鞭抽打雙飛。
為了鞭者，一尾鬃辮在鞭尖上

把氣勢削得更銳利。那時，還是一萬二千
年來，這是音波般的屏障裏
唯一的人骨折斷。鞭打即：
閃電如鞭，打下最纖細的雷聲。

黑色蛇群下地獄時，牠們的
獠牙被扣於雕花鞭柄上
只能飽嘗午間的炎熱、
汗水、流竄的後背和語言。

牠們滾起塵暴，以作報復
放逐咆哮，野獸的舒坦
與鞭觸同至。而這就
是忍受更多淨化的廟院

其後，歷經乾旱和營舍，那些
不舉的、悄語的、飄忽的傢伙
才出現，從死亡和習得中縷析
而來的技巧，就在聖瑪麗街尋到。

The Gum Forest

After the last gapped wire on a post,
homecoming for me, to enter the gum forest.

This old slow battlefield: parings of armour,
cracked collars, elbows, scattered on the ground.

New trees step out of old: lemon and ochre
splitting out of grey everywhere, in the gum forest.

In there for miles, shade track and ironbark slope,
depth casually beginning all around, at a little
    distance.

Sky sifting, and always a hint of smoke in the light;
you can never reach the heart of the gum forest.

In here is like a great yacht harbour, charmed to
    leaves,
innumerable tackle, poles wrapped in spattered sail,
or an unknown army in reserve for centuries.

Flooded-gums on creek ground, each tall because of each.
Now a blackbutt in bloom is showering with bees
but warm blood sleeps in the middle of the day.

The witching hour is noon in the gum forest.
Foliage builds like a layering splash: ground water
drily upheld in edge-on, wax-rolled, gall-puckered
leaves upon leaves. The shoal life of parrots up there.

Stone footings, trunk-shattered. Non-human lights.
Enormous abandoned machines. The mysteries of the
    gum forest.

Delight to me, though, at the water-smuggling creeks,
health to me, too, under banksia candles and combs.

A wind is up, rubbing limbs above the bullock roads;
mountains are waves in the ocean of the gum forest.

I go my way, looking back sometimes, looking round me;

singed oils clear my mind, and the pouring sound
   high up.

Why have I denied the passions of my time? To see
lightning strike upward out of the gum forest.

桉樹林

走過通電鐵線欄的最後一根木柱,
回家,對我而言,就是走入那片桉樹林。

這片古老而緩慢的戰場:裝甲刨花,
護領護肘均破裂,散落在四周。

新樹踏著老樹簇湧而出:在這片桉樹林
灰色無處不在,分裂出檸檬色和赭紅色。

樹蔭小徑和鐵皮樹山坡綿延數英里,
景深處處,始於距離稍遠的地方。

天空在篩濾,日光中總有煙靄隱約;
永遠無法達到桉樹林的心臟地帶。

於此彷彿置身於遊艇港灣,著迷於葉帆、
數不盡的索具,濺污的帆布裹著桅桿,
就像一支被養了幾個世紀的無名軍隊。

溪地上被浸淹的桉樹,競相拔高。

一棵茂盛的黑基木樹撒下一襲蜜蜂
但是正午時，溫暖的血液正在沉睡。

桉樹林裏，正午是魅惑的時刻。
葉叢疊疊，猶如層層濺灑：地面的水潭
在乾燥中苦撐，葉子輕壓葉子，
微醉，被蠟捲過，被蟲癭蛀過。樹上鸚鵡群立而生。

樹腳鋪滿石頭，樹幹已破碎。不是人造的光。
巨大的機器被廢置於此。桉樹林的玄奧。

溪流偷運水源，但是於我是愉悅，
站在猶如蠟燭和髮梳的班克西花下，於我是健爽。

一陣風起於闖牛道上，揉擦牠們的四肢；
在桉樹林之海，山巒即是海浪。

我走著自己的路，時不時回頭，環顧四周；
油輕微燎焦，讓我頭腦清淨，頭頂上還有傾瀉的
　　　聲音。

為何我拒絕生活的歡情？要看看
閃電如何從這片桉樹林煉擊天空。

The Bulldozer

The bulldozer stands short as a boot on its heel-high
    ripple soles;
it has toecapped stumps aside all day, scuffed earth and
    trampled rocks
making a hobnailed dyke downstream of raw clay shoals.
Its work will hold water. The man who bounced high
    on the box
seat, exercising levers, would swear a full frontal
    orthodox
oath to that. First he shaved off the grizzled scrub
with that front-end safety razor supplied by the school
    of hard knocks
then he knuckled down and ground his iron properly;
    they copped many a harsh rub.
At knock-off time, spilling thunder, he surfaced like a sub.

推土機

推土機像一隻立起的靴子，高卻只及腳跟，鞋底
　　波浪紋；
一整天在鞋尖般的樹樁之間穿梭，磨損泥土，踐
　　踏石頭，
把濕泥淺灘推成一個打上鞋釘的下游河堤。
它能把水圍蓄起來。一個男人跳上高高的駕駛艙，
坐下來，操控遙控桿，會毫無保留地罵出一整段
正典禱文。首先他會把斑白的矮樹叢剃平
用挫敗教育提供的前置安全剃刀。
然後他奮力工作，把鐵塊磨好，歷經許多苛刻的
　　摩輾
打盹時，暴雷突瀉，他便像潛水艇一樣冒出水面。

Poetry and Religion

Religions are poems. They concert
our daylight and dreaming mind, our
emotions, instinct, breath and native gesture

into the only whole thinking: poetry.
Nothing's said till it's dreamed out in words
and nothing's true that figures in words only.

A poem, compared with an arrayed religion,
may be like a soldier's one short marriage night
to die and live by. But that is a small religion.

Full religion is the large poem in loving repetition;
like any poem, it must be inexhaustible and complete
with turns where we ask Now why did the poet do
    that?

You can't pray a lie, said Huckleberry Finn;
you can't poe one either. It is the same mirror:
mobile, glancing, we call it poetry,

fixed centrally, we call it religion,
and God is the poetry caught in any religion,
caught, not imprisoned. Caught as in a mirror

that he attracted, being in the world as poetry
is in the poem, a law against its closure.
There'll always be religion around while there is
    poetry

or a lack of it. Both are given, and intermittent,
as the action of those birds—crested pigeon, rosella
    parrot—
who fly with wings shut, then beating, and again shut.

詩與宗教

宗教是詩，它們合謀譜寫
時光和睡夢的心，我們的
情感、本能、呼吸和天賦的姿態

把它們寫成完整的思想體系：詩。
在夢裏被轉化成語言以前，沒有言說
若只在語言裏出現，亦非真相。

一首詩，可比一場隆重的宗教儀式
也許像一個士兵短暫的新婚之夜
活與死均於此夜。但這只是小宗教。

大宗教是一首偉大的詩，有愛的重現；
就像一首詩，必須完整，且取之不盡
每一次轉折，我們都會問，為甚麼詩人這樣寫？

人無法禱告謊言。頑童費恩如是說；
人無法詩寫謊言。它們是同一面鏡子：
在遊動中瞥視，我們稱之為詩

而固定在中央，我們稱之為宗教
而上帝是被宗教抓住的詩
抓住，非囚禁。困於被祂

吸引的鏡子裏，在世上是詩
如同身處詩中，一條規則否定詩之終悟。
宗教總在身邊，身邊總有詩

或詩的缺席。兩者皆是天賦，輪換交替，
就像鳳頭鳩、玫瑰鸚鵡的動作
飛行時翅膀收起，拍一下，又收起。

The Tin Wash Dish

Lank poverty, dank poverty,
its pants wear through at fork and knee.
It warms its hands over burning shames,
refers to its fate as Them and He
and delights in things by their hard names:
rag and toejam, feed and paw—
don't guts that down, there ain't no more!
Dank poverty, rank poverty,
it hums with a grim fidelity
like wood-rot with a hint of orifice,
wet newspaper jammed in the gaps of artifice,
and disgusts us into fierce loyalty.
It's never the fault of those who love:
poverty comes down from above.
Let it dance chairs and smash the door,
it arises from all that went before
and every outsider's the enemy—
Jesus Christ turned this over with his stick
and knights and philosophers turned it back.
Rank poverty, lank poverty,

chafe in its crotch and sores in its hair,
still a window's clean if it's made of air,
not webby silver like a sleeve.
Watch out if this does well at school
and has to leave and longs to leave:
someone, sometime, will have to pay.
Shave with toilet soap, run to flesh,
astound the nation, rule the army,
still you wait for the day you'll be sent back
where books or toys on the floor are rubbish
and no one's allowed to come and play
because home calls itself a shack
and hot water crinkles in the tin wash dish.

錫洗盤

清瘦的貧窮，陰濕的貧窮，
褲子的腳叉和膝蓋穿了幾個洞。
羞恥之心燒暖了手心，
呼命運為「他們」或「他」
名字粗簡讓他滿足：
碎布、趾泥、飼料、爪子——
別吃了，都沒了！
陰濕的貧窮，階級的貧窮，
貧窮哼著歌，冷峻地盡忠
就像腐木病蝕出零星的洞，
濡濕的報紙塞滿陰謀的縫，
貧窮讓噁心，強烈地進忠。
錯總不在所愛的人身上：
只是貧窮從天而降。
讓貧窮跳椅子舞，砸破大門，
它來自過去累積的種種
每一個外人都是敵人——
耶穌基督用棍子把它挑翻
騎士和哲學家又把它還原。
階層的貧窮，清瘦的貧窮，

大腿內側的擦損，頭髮遮掩的腫痛，
乾淨的是空無一物的窗口，
好過銀飾網綴的袖口。
如果在學校表現良好，那就要小心了，
結局只有離開，甚至渴望離開：
某人某刻總要付出代價。
用廁皂剃鬚，越發虛胖，
震驚家國，統率三軍，
你仍然等著自己被遣返的一天
地板上的書籍和玩具都是垃圾
不許任何人來玩
因為家自稱陋棚
熱水在錫洗盤裏泛著漣漪。

Shellback Tick

Match-head   of groins
nailhead   in fur
blank   itch   of blank
the blood   thereof
is the strength thereof is
the jellied life-breath   is O the
sweet incision   so the curdy reed
floodeth sun-hot liquor the only ichor the only
thing which existeth wholly alley-echoing
duple rhythmic feed which same of great yore turned
my back on every other thing the mothering thereof
the seed whereof in need-clotting strings
of plaque I dissolve with reagent drool
that doth stagger swelling's occult throb.
O one tap of splendour turned to me—
blank years   grass grip
sun   haggard   rain
shell to that all.

龜殼蜱

火柴頭　　　腹股溝
釘頭　　長著毛
空白　　癢　　空白
血液　　當中
即當中的力量即
凝膠般的生命呼吸　　　O是
甜蜜的切口　　　所以乳狀的葦草
淹沒烈日般的酒，只有膿液，只有
它存在與完全小徑回聲
雙重節奏的進食，如同遠久的過去，轉過身
背對一切，當中的母愛
相關的種子，需求凝結成
血小板絲線，我與試劑流涎一起溶解
確實步履蹣跚，腫脹的詭祕的脈搏。
噢，華麗的水喉轉向我——
空白的年歲　　　緊抓住草葉
太陽　　野鷹　　雨
還得一頂龜殼以對。

Dead Trees in the Dam

Castle scaffolding tall in moat,
the dead trees in the dam
flower each morning with birds.

It can be just the three resident
cormorants with musket-hammer necks, plus
the clinician spoonbill, its long pout;

twilight's herons who were almost too lightfoot
to land; pearl galahs in pink-fronted
confederacy, each starring in its frame,

or it may be a misty candelabrum
of egrets lambent before saint Sleep—
who gutter awake and balance stiffly off.

Odd mornings, it's been all bloodflag
and rifle green: a stopped-motion shrapnel
of kingparrots. Smithereens when they freaked.

Rarely, it's wed ducks, whose children
will float among the pillars. In daytime
magpies sidestep up wood to jag pinnacles

and the big blow-in cuckoo crying
Alarm, Alarm on the wing is not let light.
This hours after dynastic charts of high

profile ibis have rowed away to beat
the paddocks. Which, however green, are
always watercolour, and on brown paper.

水塘上的枯樹

城堡棚架高高立於護城河
水塘上的枯樹
每個早上，鳥上枝頭，枯樹盛放。

可能只是三隻棲居的
鸕鷀，脖子猶如火槍擊錘，還有
一隻像臨床醫師的琵鷺，撅起長啄；

黃昏的鷺，牠們的腳纖幼得
無法落地；珍珠粉紅鳳頭鸚鵡列陣
猶如聯邦，每一隻都散發自己的光芒，

枯樹或者只是一個煙靄瀰漫的大燭臺
棲停其上的白鷺，輕輕搖曳，直至睡眠聖者——
在燭火中醒來，又僵硬地垂下。

古怪的早晨，　處處血旗
處處軍綠：一枚靜止的榴彈
藏著多少國王鸚鵡。一受驚就炸個粉碎。

鴛鴦甚少出現，牠們的雛鳥
在廊柱間漂浮。日間
喜鵲靠邊，從樹頂跳到嶙峋的岩塔

巨大的布穀鳥扇翅闖來，厲叫
警報，翅膀上的警報沒有亮起。
朝代拼圖完後，這時候高調的

朱鷺游划而去，啄食
幾片牧場。無論多麼青綠，永遠
都是牛皮紙上的水彩。

It Allows a Portrait in Line Scan at Fifteen

He retains a slight 'Martian' accent, from the years of
    single phrases.
He no longer hugs to disarm. It is gradually allowing
    him affection.
It does not allow proportion. Distress is absolute,
    shrieking, and runs him at frantic speed through
    crashing doors.
He likes cyborgs. Their taciturn power, with his
    intonation.
It still runs him around the house, alone in the dark,
    cooing and laughing.
He can read about soils, populations and New
    Zealand. On neutral topics he's illiterate.
*Arnie Schwarzenegger is an actor. He isn't a cyborg
    really, is he, Dad?*
He lives on forty acres, with animals and trees, and
    used to draw it continually.
He knows the map of Earth's fertile soils, and can
    draw it freehand.
He can only lie in a panicked shout

SorrySorryIdidn'tdoit! warding off conflict with others and himself.

When he ran away constantly it was to the greengrocers to worship stacked fruit.

His favourite country was the Ukraine: it is nearly all deep fertile soil.

Giggling, he climbed all over the dim Freudian psychiatrist who told us how autism resulted from 'refrigerator' parents.

When asked to smile, he photographs a rictus-smile on his face.

It long forbade all naturalistic films. They were Adult movies.

If they (that is, he) are bad the police will put them in hospital.

He sometimes drew the farm amid Chinese or Balinese rice terraces.

When a runaway, he made uproar in the police station, playing at three times adult speed.

Only animated films were proper. *Who Framed Roger Rabbit* then authorised the rest.

Phrases spoken to him he would take as teaching,
and repeat.

When he worshipped fruit, he screamed as if
poisoned when it was fed to him.

A one-word first conversation: *Blane.— Yes! Plane,
that's right, baby!— Blane.*

He has forgotten nothing, and remembers the precise
quality of experiences.

It requires rulings: *Is stealing very playing up, as bad
as murder?*

He counts at a glance, not looking. And he has never
been lost.

When he ate only nuts and dried fruit, words were
for dire emergencies.

He knows all the breeds of fowls, and the counties of
Ireland.

He'd begun to talk, then resumed to babble, and
silence. It withdrew speech for years.

When he took your hand, it was to work it, as a
multi-purpose tool.

He is anger's mirror, and magnifies any near him,
   raging it down.
It still won't allow him fresh fruit, or orange juice
   with bits in it.
He swam in the midwinter dam at night. It had no
   rules about cold.
He was terrified of thunder and finally cried as if in
   explanation *It—angry*!
He grilled an egg he'd broken into bread. Exchanges
   of soil-knowledge are called landtalking.
He lives in objectivity. I was sure Bell's palsy would
   leave my face only when he said it had begun to.
Don't say word! when he was eight forbade the word
   'autistic' in his presence.
Bantering questions about girlfriends cause a
   terrified look and blocked ears.
He sometimes centred the farm in a furrowed
   American Midwest.
Eye contact, Mum! means he truly wants attention. It
   dislikes I-contact.

He is equitable and kind, and only ever a little
   jealous. It was a relief when that little arrived.
He surfs, bowls, walks for miles. For many years he
   hasn't trailed his left arm while running.
I gotta get smart! looking terrified into the years. *I
   gotta get smart!*

十五歲詩畫像

他還保留著一口「火星腔」，常年説話只用
　　　短句
他已不再以擁抱來緩和敵意。它漸漸允許他
　　　擁有愛意
它不允許適可而止。焦慮肯定存在，讓他尖
　　　叫，讓他破門而出，瘋狂奔跑
他像機械人，有不苟言笑的力量和獨特的聲調
焦慮仍使他在家中奔跑，夜裏獨自大笑或咕
　　　咕地叫
他能讀懂關於新西蘭土地和人口的書，但對
　　　日常生活的話題一竅不通
「阿諾施瓦辛格是演員。他不會真的是機械
　　　人吧？是嗎？爸爸。」
他就活在四十畝範圍內，與動植物作伴，還
　　　一度繪畫這裏的景物
他把這個地球的沃壤分布圖背得滾瓜爛熟，
　　　還能徒手把它畫出來
他説謊時，只會驚慌地叫「對不起對不起不是
　　　我！」，防止對別人、對自己發起衝突
如果他經常跑出家門，肯定是去了蔬果販子

那裏參拜疊起的水果了

他最喜歡的國家是烏克蘭：幾乎整個國家都是
　　肥沃的土壤

他一邊笑，一邊爬到弗洛伊德派的心理醫生身
　　上，

醫生告訴我們「雪櫃型」家長導致子女患上
　　自閉症

別人叫他笑，他會掛出一幅標準的露齒笑容

他早就不看自然主義電影了，因為那是大人的
　　影片

「如果他們是壞人，警察會送他們去醫
　　院。」他其實在說自己

有時他把家裏的農場畫到中國或巴厘島的稻米
　　梯田上

玩越獄餘生時，他會以三倍於成人的速度跑到
　　警察局咆哮

只有動畫片才適合他看，有《誰陷害了兔子羅
　　傑》就甚麼都行

他會把對他說的隻言片語當成教導，把它們一
　　遍一遍地念

他參拜水果時，如果你讓他吃，他會尖叫起
　　來，彷彿水果有毒
一次單詞對話：「灰機」「對！飛機。説得真
　　好！」「灰機」
他甚麼也沒有忘記，還準確地記得經歷的特質
他還要裁定：「盜竊真的讓人那麼生氣嗎？和
　　謀殺一樣嗎？」
他以瞥視來認路，而不是細心地觀望，但他從
　　未迷路
他只吃果仁和乾果時，説話已是十萬火急的
　　信號
他熟知所有家禽種類和所有愛爾蘭郡縣
他開始説話，然後喋喋不休，最後沉默。收
　　回幾年來所説的話
當他牽起你的手，他是要使用這個多功能工
　　具
他是一塊映出憤怒的鏡子，會放大身邊的怒
　　氣，又用怒氣把它平息
它仍不讓他吃新鮮水果，不讓他喝帶果肉的
　　果汁

寒天夜裏，他會跑去水塘裏游泳。它對寒冷毫
　　無規則可言

雷聲會把他嚇到，他會大叫「它：憤氣！」彷
　　彿在解釋

他把雞蛋打到麵包上，然後烤著吃。交流關於
　　土壤的知識會被稱作「地說」

他活在客觀的世界，只有他說面癱離我而去
　　了，我會才相信

「別說！」他八歲時，不讓我們說「自閉」
　　二字

開起找女朋友的玩笑，會讓他露出懼色，閉起
　　耳朵

有時，他會把我們的農場畫到美國中西部的耕
　　地上

「媽，看眼睛！」意思是，他真的需要關注，
　　但不喜歡主動看你

他為人公正，友善，只是有時有點嫉妒。一丁
　　點嫉妒卻是一種解放

他划水，滾地，走幾英里。多年來，他奔跑時
　　都不會放鬆左臂

「我要聰明起來！」想到未來，他很害怕。

「我要聰明起來！」

Deaf Language

Two women were characters, continually
rewriting themselves, in turn, with their hands
mostly, but with face and torso too
and very fast, in brushwork like the gestures
above a busy street in Shanghai.

聾語

兩位女子就是文字，不斷
輪流重寫自己，通常
用手，也會用臉和上身
非常迅速，身姿猶若
上海繁華的街道上
兩支揮舞的毛筆。

A Postcard

A mirrory tar-top road across
a wide plain. Drizzling sky.
A bike is parked at a large book
turned down tent-fashion on the verge.
One emerging says *I read such crazy*
things in this book. 'Every bird
has stone false teeth and enters
the world in its coffin.' That's in there.

一張明信片

一條鏡子般的瀝青路穿過
廣袤的平原。天在下著毛毛雨。
一輛單車泊在一本大書旁邊
書在路邊，被反過來，像帳篷。
有人冒出來說，我從這本書裏
讀到這種荒謬的事：「每一隻鳥
都有石頭做的假牙，乘著棺具
進入這個世界。」就在這裏面。

The Images Alone

Scarlet as the cloth draped over a sword,
white as steaming rice, blue as leschenaultia,
old curried towns, the frog in its green human skin;
a ploughman walking his furrow as if in irons, but
as at a whoop of young men running loose
in brick passages, there occurred the thought
like instant stitches all through crumpled silk:

as if he'd had to leap to catch the bullet.

A stench like hands out of the ground.
The willows had like beads in their hair, and
Peenemünde, grunted the dentist's drill, Peenemünde!
Fowls went on typing on every corn key, green
kept crowding the pinks of peach trees into the sky
but used speech balloons were tacky in the river
and waterbirds had liftoff as at a repeal of gravity.

意象罷了

紅，如劍上的抹布；
白，如熱騰騰的米飯；藍，如初戀草。
馬櫛梳理的老鎮，青蛙披上綠色人皮
農夫與犁溝同行，彷彿在鐵具上，但是
年輕人發出一聲叫喊，發足亂跑
在石磚走道上，突然有一個念頭
就像縫針瞬間穿過皺褶的絲綢：

彷彿他必須跳起來接住一粒子彈。

一股惡臭，就像從地面伸出的手。
楊柳，彷彿頭髮掛著水珠，還有
佩內明德鎮，牙醫電鑽咕嚕，佩內明德鎮！
家禽繼續敲打玉米鍵盤，綠色
不斷包圍桃樹的粉紅，延伸到天空
但是用過的對話框在河流裏如此俗氣
水鳥發射起飛，就像向萬有引力提出上訴

The Moon Man

Shadowy kangaroos moved off
as we drove into the top paddock
coming home from a wedding
under a midnightish curd sky

then his full face cleared:
Moon man, the first birth ever
who still massages his mother
and sends her light, for his having

been born fully grown.
His brilliance is in our blood.
Had Earth fully healed from that labour
no small births could have happened.

月人

袋鼠影影綽綽地跳過
我們駕車往地勢最高的牧場
參加完婚禮，走在回家的路上
半夜的天空如同乳膠

他的整張臉變得很清楚：
月人，世上第一位
他仍為母親按摩
給她點火，因為他

一出生就是成年。
他的光芒在我們的血液裏。
如果地球已從這次生產中復元
一切生產就不會被説成渺小了。

The Great Cuisine Cleaver Dance Sonnet

Juice-wet black steel
rectangle with square bite
dock pork slice slice
candy pork mouth size
heel-and-toe work walk
thru greens wad widths
bloc duck bisect bone
facet glaze nick snake
slit wriggle take gallbladder
whop garlic shave lily-root
wham! clay chicken-crust
hiss wok plug flare
circling soy cringing prawn
blade amassing sideways mince.

切工廚師之舞十四行詩

沾滿果汁的黑鋼刀
四方均有銳角
碼頭豬肉片片
糖果豬肉口口
踵趾步腳下功夫
菜葉成捆，手起刀落
鴨肉成塊，對分開骨
刀面油亮，細雕蛇身
游弋刀鋒挑膽囊
拍蒜頭，批藕皮
威風！炸雞麵衣如泥
嘶，鍋，堵，火
旋刮黃豆，對蝦痙攣
刀鋒積累，刀邊肉碎

The Poisons of Right and Left

You are what you have got
and: to love, you have to hate.
Two ideas that have killed and maimed
holocausts and myriads.

左右之毒

你是你之所有
去愛就必須恨
兩者互殺相殘
大屠殺千百萬

Death from Exposure

That winter. We missed her stark face
at work. Days till she was found, under

his verandah. Even student torturers
used to go in awe. She had zero small talk.

It made no sense she had his key.
It made no sense all she could have

done. Depression exhausts the mind.
She phones, no response, she drives up

straight to his place in the mountains,
down a side road, frost all day.

You knock. What next? You can't manage
what next. Back at last, he finds her car.

She's crawled in, under, among the firewood.
Quite often the world is not round.

曝光致死

那年冬天，我們想念她
工作時僵硬的臉。想起那些

在門廊找到她的日子。甚至折磨學生的人
也曾一臉敬畏地趕過去。她從不說廢話。

不可能啊，她有他家的鑰匙。
不可能啊，她怎麼做成那麼多

事情。抑鬱已榨乾的她的心神。
她打電話，沒人接，她開車

上山，直接到他的家去，
開過一條整天結著霜的小路。

你敲門。接下來呢？接下來
你無法控制。他終於回來了，看到她的車。

她爬進了，進去，滿身柴火
地球往往不是圓的。

The Farm Terraces

Beautiful merciless work
around slopes of earth
terraces cut by curt hoe
at the orders of hunger
or a pointing lord.
Levels eyed up to rhyme
copied from grazing animals
round the steeps of earth,
balconies filtering water
down stage to stage of drop.
Wind-stirred colours of crop
swell between walked bunds
miles of grass-rimmed contour
harvests down from the top
by hands long in the earth.
Baskets of rich made soil
boosted up poor by the poor,
ladder by freestone prop
stanzas of chant-long lines
by backwrenching slog, before

money, gave food and drunk
but rip now like slatted sails
(some always did damn do)
down the abrupts of earth.

梯田

漂亮而殘忍的傑作
在傾斜的土坡上
短鋤頭掘出梯田
下命令的是飢餓
還是指指戳戳的地主
層層向尾韻看齊
模仿吃著草的動物
在傾斜的土坡上
露臺過濾掉的水
從舞臺流落水滴的舞臺
莊稼有被風翻起的顏色
在海邊馬路之間膨脹
草圍起數英里長的輪廓
在土地上，躬身臂長
從最高的梯田收割下來
籃子裏都是人造沃壤
攀比誰比誰更窮
砂岩撐起一把梯
詩節的詩行長如聖頌
幹斷背脊的苦活，金錢

未賺到，便吃喝揮霍
但是撕開來像頁帆片片
　（總有人幹下去）
落入土地的深淵。

萊斯·馬雷，著名澳洲詩人，生於1938年10月，1965年開始發表詩歌，至今出版超過16本詩集。他居住在新南威爾士州本雅鄉的農場，即是他出生的地方。馬雷的詩曾被翻譯成德文、荷蘭文、丹麥文、挪威文、瑞典文、法文、意大利文、斯洛文尼亞文、馬其頓文和西班牙文等，在世界各地出版，並贏得許多國際詩歌獎，包括「格蕾絲利文詩歌獎」、「皮特拉克詩歌獎」、「英國皇后詩歌金章」、「T.S.艾略特詩歌獎」、「意大利蒙德約國際詩歌獎」等。在馬雷的作品中，衝突的主題多出現於早年他在城市時寫的詩，回歸鄉野後，他嘗試抵抗都市題材的誘惑。

Les Murray, born October 1938, is a prominent Australian poet who has published 16 poetry collections since 1965. He lives on a small former farm at Bunyah, the rural district in which he grew up. Some of his collections have been published in translation, notably in German, Dutch, Danish, Norwegian, Swedish, French, Italian, Slovenian, Macedonian and Spanish, and he has won notable prizes in several of the listed languages. Prominent prizes in English that have come his way home have included the Petrarch Prize, the T. S. Eliot Prize, Queen's Gold Medal for Poetry and the Mondello Prize in Italy. Conflict is a diminishing theme in his writing, and plays a lesser role now than in earlier years, being set aside very largely by subjects of rural life and the Lord. He has tended to resist urgings to concentrate on urban subjects.

出版 Publisher
香港中文大學出版社 The Chinese University Press

封面影像 Cover Image
北島 Bei Dao

出版日期 Date of Publication
二零一五年十一月 November 2015

國際書號 ISBN
978-962-996-723-9

香港國際詩歌之夜 2015 International Poetry Nights in Hong Kong 2015
主辦單位 Organizer
香港中文大學文學院 Faculty of Arts, The Chinese University of Hong Kong

協辦單位 Co-organizers
香港中文大學中國文化研究所
Institute of Chinese Studies, The Chinese University of Hong Kong
香港中文大學出版社 The Chinese University Press
香港兆基創意書院 HKICC Lee Shau Kee School of Creativity
廣州時刻文化傳播有限公司 Moment Communications

贊助 Sponsors
香港法國文化協會 Alliance Française de Hong Kong
上海廿一文化發展有限公司 Shanghai 21 Culture Promotion Co., Ltd.
中國會 The China Club
香港文學出版社有限公司 The Hong Kong Literary Press Co. Limited
斑馬谷文化發展 (北京) 有限公司 Zebra Valley Culture Development